Real life, real answers.

The easy family budget

- Save 5%
- Transaction log
- Basic Money mgment course

Real life, real answers.

The easy family budget

by
Jerald W. Mason

Houghton Mifflin Company   Boston
1990

For information about permission to reproduce selections from this book, write to
Permissions, Houghton Mifflin Company, 2 Park Street, Boston, Massachusetts
02108.

Library of Congress Catalog Card Number: 89-85913
ISBN: 0-395-51096-1

General editors: Barbara Binswanger, James Charlton, Lee Simmons

Design by Hudson Studio

"Real life, real answers" is a trademark of the John Hancock Mutual Life Insurance
Company.

Printed in the United States of America

10 9 8 7 6 5 4 3 2 1

Although this book is designed to provide accurate and authoritative information in
regard to the subject matter covered, neither the author and general editors nor the
publisher are engaged in rendering legal, accounting, or other professional service.
If legal advice or other expert assistance is required, the services of a competent
professional should be sought.

Contents

Introduction

B udget. The word may make you as uncomfortable as the thought of undergoing a tax audit, speaking in public, or root canal work. But it doesn't have to be that way. A well-conceived budget—one with which you and your family can live—will change your life for the better.

> **Tip:** If the word "budget" is itself a stumbling block for you, call your budget a "spending plan," a "money management system," or a "financial system." This might strike you as silly, but if it helps you take that first step toward achieving your goals...do it.

The basic purpose of this book is to help you become a better money manager. It is written to show you how to make your income go further. The solution to most people's money problems is not making more money, but knowing how to manage what they have.

Money does indeed make the world go around. It largely determines where and how you live, how you spend your leisure time, and all those elements that make up what is commonly known as your lifestyle. Money also affects your self-esteem. Your personal aspirations and dreams for the future are tied to your financial situation.

If you feel, as so many do, that money, or a lack of it, controls you, it is time to play animal trainer. Take the bull by the horns and get the monkey off your back.

Consider the following questions:

- ☐ Does it seem like you never have enough money?
- ☐ Are you able to save money regularly?
- ☐ Are you carrying a debt load that feels overwhelming?
- ☐ Do you have any "umbrella" money put away for a rainy day?
- ☐ Do you have outstanding bills that are overdue?
- ☐ Are you able to fund goals that are important to you?
- ☐ Do you anticipate financial needs well?
- ☐ Are you an impulsive shopper?
- ☐ Do you frequently use credit because you are short of cash?
- ☐ Are your financial records efficient and up to date?
- ☐ Do you have a system for keeping track of credit card purchases and automatic teller machine (ATM) withdrawals?
- ☐ Is your credit rating as strong as it could be?

These questions are not meant to depress you. With a budget that you tailor to your needs, you can gain control of your finances. As you get your expenditures in line and build a nest egg, your self-esteem will soar.

This book will help you work out a spending plan that is sensible, realistic, and manageable. We will proceed one step at a time. So kick off your shoes, settle into a comfortable chair, and read on.

CHAPTER I

Know thyself

B efore you sharpen those No. 2 pencils and crack open the checkbook, let's examine the most important element in developing your financial system: you. You must take a close look at who you are, what your goals are, and how you expect to fund those goals.

BASIC ISSUES

While you will make millions of decisions during your lifetime, some will be more critical than others. Your decisions on four issues will have the most impact on your finances.

1. Profession and level of education. Job satisfaction is profoundly important to most people. If you are dissatisfied with your job or are looking to improve your income, you may need to return to school. That requires time and money.

2. Home ownership. Don't fall into the trap of equating monthly mortgage payments with the cost of owning a home. A monthly mortgage payment is about 50 percent of the annual cost of owning a home. You must also factor in property taxes, utilities, insurance, repairs, improvements, and landscaping. And don't forget you have to furnish the place, too. Buy a house you can afford.

3. Children. As any parent will tell you, kids cost money. Have you priced sneakers lately? Gone are the days when a big, healthy brood to work the farm was an asset. The cost of raising one child today ranks just behind buying a home or funding retirement. The real financial geniuses of this century are those parents who can figure out how to afford more than two kids. Remember, children demand an enormous financial commitment.

4. Retirement. While it is true that more Americans than ever are retiring with adequate incomes, many more are outliving those incomes. Many of those who retire in their late fifties and early sixties will find that by their mid-seventies, their primary sources of income have become Social Security and welfare.

These issues must be addressed with great care and forethought. If your budget is hard to balance because your salary is low, you own too much house, you have a big family, or your retirement funds are dwindling, there is no easy solution. But take heart. Time is on your side. For example:

☐ You can return to school and qualify for a better paying job. There are dozens of programs to help you. Check with your local department of education regarding high school equivalency programs, community college courses, and continuing education services.

☐ You can take the equity you have in your house and reinvest it in a more moderately priced home that will suit you just as well.

☐ Your children will grow up, move out, and find jobs. They might require a little nudge when it comes time to leave the nest, but eventually they will fly solo.

☐ You can qualify for state aid and federal assistance if, as a retiree, you are having financial difficulties.

EVALUATING YOUR SITUATION

A successful spending plan, in large part, depends upon your age and family situation. You probably fall into one of the following categories.

Young, single, and childless

There are fewer demands on you financially than on your friends who have children. Your paycheck is rising steadily as you pursue your career. But you do have expenses: paying off a student loan, buying your first car, furnishing an apartment. You must remember: Single people have a hard time saving money and often find they have negative net worths (their liabilities outnumber their assets). Start putting aside a little bit each pay period now so you can eventually afford the down payment on a condominium, co-op, or house. Saving for long-term goals? It's hard enough deciding what to have for dinner. Who can think that far into the future? You can. Why? Because it's smart and it pays off. Put away 5 percent of your income now. If you start saving in your twenties, by the time you turn sixty every dollar you put away could be worth eight to ten times as much as dollars you start saving in your forties.

While you are providing only for yourself, make saving money a habit. Your peers might be living for today; you live for today while putting a little away for tomorrow.

DINKS

If you are a DINK (dual income, no kids) couple, the demands of two careers and the rewards of two salaries combine to make spending a lot easier than saving. You probably dine out far more frequently than friends who have children. You take more vacations and spend more on clothes and expensive "adult toys" as well. Getting your finances under control with a budget should be a priority, because your ability to save money for long-term goals will never be greater. You should be saving at least 10 percent of your combined incomes.

Another *Real life, real answers* book, *Financial planning for the two-career family*, offers specific advice for couples, either with or without children, who both work.

Married with children

You know kids are expensive. Skateboards with state of the art wheels; orthodontists; ballet classes; horseback riding lessons; and on and on.

Real life, real answers.

Pam and Jed Smith relocated from Boston to St. Louis because of Pam's promotion. Housing was much more affordable in the Midwest. They felt the time had arrived for them to own their dream home. Within a week of their arrival, they bought a Tudor-style, four-bedroom house on five beautifully tended acres. Pam and Jed were thrilled. However, they didn't take the time to consider the price tags on utilities, insurance, property taxes, and new furniture. These costs were significantly higher than what they had been in Boston because the Smiths had purchased a much larger house. They thought Pam's raise would cover the additional costs. But the truth soon became obvious. They had bought too much house. The Smiths put themselves on a tight budget with the expectation that over time inflation and salary increases would ease their burden.

Start a college fund as soon as possible. If your child decides not to go to college, the worst that can happen is that you have saved a small nest egg to use as you choose.

Remember to budget money for special needs such as eyeglasses, braces, lessons, special recreational activities, and summer camp.

Mature couples and individuals

Your children have children of their own and you have paid off your mortgage. It's time to check on your savings for retirement. A session with a financial planner or an insurance or investment adviser is recommended. You need to save and invest a significant portion of your monthly income. Tax-sheltered retirement plans such as the 401(k), an IRA, or an annuity should be considered. Review your medical coverage. Learn about long-term care policies now. Carefully analyze your financial situation before you stop working.

Retirees

You retired on what seemed to be an adequate income, but now you are feeling the pinch. Be sure your medical coverage is up to date and sufficient. Keep to your spending plan. Wise retirees continue saving money for rainy day needs.

MAKING BETTER FINANCIAL DECISIONS

You are almost ready to develop your budget. But before you start crunching numbers, you need to focus in greater detail on how you make financial decisions.

☐ How well do you make spending decisions?
☐ Do those decisions consistently conform to your financial objectives?
☐ Are you an impulse buyer?
☐ What motivates you to shop?
☐ How much are you buying on credit?
☐ Do you regret some of the financial decisions you've made in the last year?
☐ Have you made important decisions haphazardly or even recklessly?

Poor financial decisions are easy to make. People often spend more time choosing a movie than they do planning a major purchase.

There is a lesson here: Take time when you make a crucial financial decision. Plan ahead, do research, and be realistic.

To help you make better financial decisions, take the following quiz. Select something expensive from your personal wish list as the item you want to buy. Let's use a sailboat as an example.

☐ What is motivating you to make this purchase?
☐ What are you gaining and what are you giving up if you buy the sailboat?
☐ Will your budget accommodate the hefty price tag?

- [ ] Will your budget be able to withstand repairs, upkeep, insurance, and storage fees?
- [ ] Do you have to use credit to complete the transaction?
- [ ] If you put off the decision to buy for a day or two, will the desire to own the boat lessen?
- [ ] Would you be better off renting a boat on the weekends when you want to sail?
- [ ] Can you buy a used boat?
- [ ] Do you and your spouse or partner agree on the purchase?
- [ ] How much research have you done?

Tip: Your neighborhood librarian can help you find published evaluations of just about any product or service. Research saves you money and results in a purchase that fits your needs.

- [ ] Will the satisfaction you receive from buying this boat counterbalance what you will feel as you write the monthly check to the creditor?
- [ ] Will owning this boat make you (or someone close to you) happier?

These questions may seem tough. They are meant to be. Major financial decisions cannot be made lightly. The couples in the *Real life, real answers* example on page 10 handled the issue of big purchases differently but effectively.

One of these systems might work for you (adjust the dollar amount to fit your needs). For every "deal of the century" you miss because you did not act NOW—there will be money in your pocket because of all the bad deals you pass up.

DETERMINING YOUR GOALS

Now it is time to think about your goals. You cannot create a workable budget without first making a list of the goals you hope to fund.

The following exercise will help you identify what is really important to you. (If you are married, ask your spouse to complete this exercise also; then compare lists.)

Look over the following list. These are general goals you may be working toward. Fill in the blanks with a "1" if the goal is extremely important to you, a "2" if the goal is somewhat important, and a "3" if it does not have a high priority.

PRIORITY LIST

_1_ Owning your own home.

_3_ Owning a vacation home.

_2_ Obtaining additional education.

_3_ Owning a luxury car.

_1_ Getting out of debt.

_1_ Having adequate insurance.

_3_ Saving for retirement.

_3_ Being able to work fewer hours per week.

_3_ Paying for your child's college education.

_2_ Enjoying your work more.

_2_ Having more time for your hobbies.

_1_ Better controlling your finances.

_3_ Starting your own business.

_2_ Traveling.

_1_ Building an investment portfolio.

___ _____

___ _____

___ _____

Now take a minute and focus on those goals that earned a rating of 1. Do you really devote more of your time and money to achieving those goals than those that received a 2 or a 3? If not, why not? You may need to spend some time sorting out your basic priorities before you decide on more specific goals.

Real life, real answers.

Anya and Martin Chan used to disagree over virtually every purchase one made without consulting the other. Martin suggested a trial arrangement. If either planned on making a purchase over $30, they would discuss it first. If they could not agree, they would forgo the purchase. The plan proved an ideal solution. After a few months, they found they only needed to confer on items over $100. They are now up to $250 and are delighted with the success of Martin's plan.

Hedy and Ed Cooper found they often regretted their important financial decisions. They were impulse buyers. Driving by a car showroom, Ed's eye was caught by a green sports coupe. He spun into the lot to have a closer look. Hedy and Ed had often fantasized about owning a jazzy little car, so they bought it on the spot. The next morning they knew they had made a mistake in buying the car so hastily. Hedy suggested they set up the following procedure to help curb their financial recklessness.

- Do not make single purchases between $200 and $500 without taking a day to "sleep on it."
- Delay making purchases between $500 and $1,000 for two days.
- Ponder purchases between $1,000 and $10,000 for three days.
- Consider anything over $10,000 for a full week.

CREATING A GOAL SCHEDULE

If you are single and without children, you can start on your goal list. If, however, you are married, have a live-in partner, or have a family, call a family council.

Tip: If you don't already do it, make a habit of holding regular family councils. Everyone should have the chance to speak his or her mind. Don't be nervous about discussing finances in front of your children. They enjoy being included and it's the best "on-the-job training" they'll ever get.

Ask each member of the family to list both individual and family goals. This will be an enlightening experience—for everyone. Each will learn how to negotiate, compromise, stand up for himself or herself, and make decisions. If everyone is involved in creating the Family Goal List, everyone will have a vested interest in supporting the goals.

Now fill in the Goal Schedule that follows below (an example has been entered for you). Use a pencil with a good eraser because you will want to list your goals according to priority. This will take some thought. Use your Priority List as a draft.

GOAL SCHEDULE

Date:

Goal	Target Date	Start Saving	Dollar Amount	No. of Deposits	Monthly Deposit
College fund	9/2000	9/1992	$20,000	96 (8 years x 12 months)	$208
pay off Cr					
pay off bank					
CAR					

Column 1. Briefly describe each goal as specifically as possible. Remember to list goals in order of priority.

Column 2. When do you want to have funds available to

achieve the goal? Write in the month and the year.

Column 3. When can you start funding each goal? Write in the month and the year.

Column 4. Estimate what each goal would cost if paid for today. Inflation will probably increase the price tag when it comes time to meet your goal. But remember, the money you set aside to fund the goal is also growing (earning interest or dividends). Pessimists might argue that you will need to pay taxes on the interest or dividends. But the number of dollars you have saved (even after paying taxes) should about equal the cost of achieving the goal.

Column 5. How many months are there between the month and year when you can start funding and the month and year when the money is required?

Column 6. Divide the costs of each of the goals in column 4 by the number of months in column 5. The result is what you need to save or invest each month.

TECHNIQUES FOR SAVING

How successful have you been in funding your goals in the past? Getting your income to cover your monthly expenses seems challenging enough. This is where an important technique comes into play: *Pay yourself first.*

You may have heard of this technique before. But have you tried it? The following two strategies make the "pay yourself first" rule work.

1. Make it as easy as you can to deposit money into savings and investment accounts. Consider asking your employer to withhold money from your paycheck and deposit the amount into a 401(k) account, or use the funds to buy Series EE Savings Bonds. You won't miss money you never see. Or have your bank transfer money from your checking account to a savings or investment account automatically a day after your payroll check has cleared. Giving a mutual fund permission to write a check against your checking account once a month is another possibility.

2. Make it as difficult as you can to get at the money. If it is easy to withdraw money from the account, you will. Money taken from a 401(k) before you reach retirement age will be subjected to a 10 percent penalty. If you cash in Series EE Bonds before they mature, you will lose interest. Some people save money in accounts several states away because they can get money out of the account only by writing a letter to the bank. Put your money in a safe place, but make it difficult to reach.

> **Tip:** The size of the initial payment you make doesn't matter. If you can put aside only a modest amount, do it. You can increase the amount by saving a larger percentage of your next pay raise or, when you next pay off a loan, continue depositing that payment into a savings account.

As you manage your money more effectively, you will find ways to increase your monthly savings. Remember, time is your ally.

The chart below shows how little amounts grow into large amounts when savings are made each month. If you were to save $10 a month and could earn 5 or 9 percent on your money, you would have the following amounts after 5, 10, 20, or 40 years.

SAVING $10 A MONTH AT 5% AND 9% INTEREST RATES

Years	5%	9%
5	$682	$759
10	$1,559	$1,949
20	$4,127	$6,728
40	$15,323	$47,167

Obviously, money grows much faster at 9 percent than it does at 5 percent. And because of the magic of compounding, interest earns interest. Your money grows faster the longer it is left in the account.

You have come quite a distance already and done a little soul-searching along the way. Now it's time to develop your spending plan.

Tip: Keep in mind that the fundamental principle of budgeting is simple: Spend less than you earn and save and invest the rest. It's not effortless, but it is attainable.

CHAPTER II

Getting started

The key to financial peace of mind is a budget, and successful budgeting requires a certain amount of patience and commitment. Once you begin following a spending plan tailored to your needs, you will be able to reduce impulse buying, control overspending, create emergency funds, fund your goals, and have money left over to start a wealth-building program.

Whether or not you have ever budgeted before, you do have a pattern for spending money.

Budgets do not have to be complicated. And they do not have to reduce you to pinching pennies or trying to account for every dime. Budgeting is a tool to help you spend money thoughtfully and save money wisely. A good budget is one that isn't written in stone. A successful budgeter has the discipline to stick to the plan and make adjustments as experience dictates.

 Tip: Budgets have to be realistic. Be sure to take into account the feelings of each member of the household before you develop the final blueprint for a budget.

But do not underestimate the amount of work that goes into developing a budget. This is a big job. Take your time, be honest with yourself, and let's begin.

First things first. Clear off your work space (a big table top is best because you can spread out) and gather everything you need before you sit down to start working. Like any good craftsperson, you should line up your tools before you start the job:

- ☐ A calculator.
- ☐ Ledger sheets (available at stationery stores).
- ☐ Notepads.
- ☐ Sharpened pencils with good erasers and a sharpener.
- ☐ Paperclips.
- ☐ A stapler.
- ☐ Separate files for paid and unpaid bills.
- ☐ Your list of goals.
- ☐ Check stubs for the last 12 months.
- ☐ Credit card charge statements for the last 12 months.
- ☐ Automatic teller machine statements for the last 12 months.
- ☐ Records of medical expenses and insurance.
- ☐ Pay stubs for the last 12 months.
- ☐ A copy of your most recent state and federal income tax returns.
- ☐ Any other financial records you have been keeping.
- ☐ Your business diary.

Tip: Indulge yourself with some attractive file folders and snappy supplies. Keep them together in a shoebox so you don't have to round them up each time you sit down to work on the budget. (But don't go overboard. After all, you're on a budget!)

If you are adept on your home computer, by all means use it. There are dozens of software programs available. Find one you like, especially if it is designed to help you with your income taxes at the end of the year. Remember to make a backup copy of your work.

Work at a time that's best for you, such as a quiet morning when you are feeling refreshed. Eliminate distractions.

Real life, real answers.

E ~~than Shaw~~ *Sue Wilson* deposits his salary in a checking account and then writes checks until the balance is zero. If the check register shows a zero balance, he uses credit cards or overdraft privileges to see him through until his next payday. He has fallen into the habit of paying the minimum monthly requirement on his credit cards. Ethan has no idea where his money goes.

Ethan Shaw's method is one extreme. Chuck Matthews's is the other. Chuck Matthews means well. He has developed an intricate system that requires hours of bookkeeping each month. The system is complicated, idiosyncratic, and anxiety-producing. He has come to resent his own system and so puts off using it. For all of his files and logbooks, he spends too much time making his system work while ignoring the actual budget.

THE CHALLENGES OF BUDGETING

You will need to estimate as accurately as possible all sources and uses of income for the next 12 months. It is easy to forget some expenditures. At first you will underestimate the dollar amount of several expenditures. Because inflation is a part of our lives, some expenditures will increase in cost over the next 12 months. Few, if any, will decrease.

Cash expenditures are particularly hard to estimate. As an exercise, carry around a notebook or diary for a week or longer. Write down precisely how you spend your money. Make your entries several times a day to ensure an accurate and, therefore, meaningful record. Keep Post-it notes in your wallet and/or diary. This will remind you to write down purchases you make.

Keeping a record of how you spend your money is a difficult task but a valuable lesson and an eye-opening experience. Get into the habit of asking for receipts. They will help you keep track of your spending and be helpful during tax time.

Your budget must balance. There must be enough income to cover all expenditures. For most people it is easier to reduce expenditures than to increase income when trying to balance a budget. You may not want to find out if you have enough money to cover your expenses. The "head-in-the-sand" approach must be overcome. Budgeting demands that you be honest, with yourself, your spouse, your family, and your creditors.

You must save part of your income to fund future goals. This is difficult for most people. However, if you don't list specific goals in your budget, they won't get funded.

Most people feel they have too much debt. If you are suffering from debt overload, you know what a tight budget feels like. Isn't it time to stop creating more debt?

A budget can cover any length of time. Most are for 12 months. However, it need not run from January to December. Remember, certain expenses are not consistent from month to month. To estimate a monthly amount for your budget, simply divide the amount spent annually on such items by 12.

Once the budget worksheet on page 26 has been completed, it will give you an idea of where your money comes from and how you plan to spend it. This is the core of your budget.

Use a pencil to record each estimate, since you will probably change many of them. The more complete your prior records are, the closer each estimate will be to what you will actually earn and spend.

Tip: There is a tendency to overestimate income while underestimating expenses when working out a spending plan. Be wary.

ESTIMATING INCOME

Use the chart that follows on pages 19 to 20 to identify all income sources and amounts. Then transfer the information to the worksheet on page 26. Include as many sources as you can. Review your check stubs, bank statements, and last year's

Real life, real answers.

G ary Perez is a sales representative for a lumber exporter. His income varies and is somewhat seasonal. Several years ago (when his finances seemed to have a life of their own) Gary decided to try budgeting. He set up his spending plan using conservative estimates as to what he expected to earn each month. When his income exceeded his estimates, he deposited the difference into a money market account. Occasionally, when he made less than what he targeted, he transferred funds from the money market account to his checking account. When the balance in the money market account exceeded $10,000, he invested the extra money in a mutual fund. His finances are now well under control.

income tax return. If you are not a salaried employee, accurately estimating your income can be a challenge. Be conservative.

SOURCES OF CASH   AMOUNTS

☐ Sue's   's salary/wages.   _____

☐ _____'s salary/wages.   _____

☐ Stock/mutual fund
   dividends.   _____

☐ Interest (bonds, CDs,
   money market funds).   _____

☐ Rent.   _____

☐ Disability income.   _____

☐ Social Security.   _____

☐ Aid to Families with
   Dependent Children (AFDC).   _____

☐ Alimony.   _____

☐ Child support.   _____

☐ Annuity.	_____
☐ Company pension.	_____
☐ Bonus.	_____
☐ Commission.	_____
☐ Tips.	_____
☐ IRA/Keogh.	_____
☐ Workers' compensation.	_____
☐ Tax refunds.	_____
☐ Sale of assets.	_____
☐ Interest on savings.	_____
☐ Loans and monies borrowed.	_____
☐ _____	_____
☐ _____	_____
☐ _____	_____
☐ _____	_____

This list suggests the most common sources of income. You may have other sources. Include everything.

ESTIMATING EXPENSES

If you have been keeping records, you should have a reasonable idea of where your money goes. If you have no idea, now is the time for the little diary that was mentioned earlier. You may need to write everything down for two or three months before you start to have a picture of your spending habits. Such a diary—in addition to your check register, old bills, and last year's tax return—will be helpful in identifying the different types of expenses. Fill in the following chart and then transfer the information to the worksheet on page 26.

TAXES

AMOUNTS

- ☐ Federal income taxes
  and withholding taxes. _____
- ☐ Federal estimated taxes. _____
- ☐ Social Security (FICA). _____
- ☐ State income taxes. _____
- ☐ City/county income taxes. _____
- ☐ Real estate property taxes. _____
- ☐ Personal property taxes
  (auto, furniture, etc.). _____
- ☐ _____ _____

GOALS

By now you have an idea about the financial goals you wish to achieve. Go back to your list of goals on page 11 and list those you believe you can fund during the next 12 months. You may have to eliminate one or more goals when you balance your budget.

- ☐ 401(k) or 403(b) "TSA." _____
- ☐ IRA/Keogh. _____
- ☐ Education. _____
- ☐ Children's tuition. _____
- ☐ Down payment on a home. _____
- ☐ Investment portfolio. _____
- ☐ Trip. _____
- ☐ Cars/boats/bikes. _____
- ☐ Emergency fund. _____
- ☐ _____ _____

DEBTS

This list may be longer than you would like, but include all debts.

- ☐ Home mortgage(s). _____
- ☐ Auto loan(s). _____
- ☐ Credit cards: annual fees
  and purchases. _____
- ☐ Medical bills. _____
- ☐ Installment loans. _____
- ☐ Personal loans. _____
- ☐ Bank loans. _____
- ☐ Home equity lines of credit. _____
- ☐ Life insurance loans. _____
- ☐ _____ _____

CONTRACTS

You are legally obligated to pay contractual expenses. Examples are alimony, child support, college loans, insurance premiums, and utilities.

- ☐ Life insurance. _____
- ☐ Family life insurance. _____
- ☐ Property insurance. _____
- ☐ Auto insurance. _____
- ☐ Umbrella liability insurance. _____
- ☐ Medical insurance. _____
- ☐ Disability insurance. _____
- ☐ Dental. _____
- ☐ Hospital. _____

- ☐ Electricity. _____
- ☐ Natural gas. _____
- ☐ Garbage. _____
- ☐ Water. _____
- ☐ Sewer. _____
- ☐ Cable TV. _____
- ☐ Rent. _____
- ☐ Furniture rental. _____
- ☐ Child support. _____
- ☐ Alimony. _____
- ☐ _____ _____

DAY-TO-DAY EXPENSES

When balancing a budget, most people begin by trying to reduce day-to-day expenses: They are the easiest to cut when you have to economize. Therefore, you may want to list your day-to-day expenses in order of importance, with the most important, such as food and housing, first.

These expenses are harder to estimate. Though you may have a good idea about how much you need for taxes, goals, and contractual obligations, daily expenses are more difficult to calculate. Here again, an efficient recordkeeping system is essential to know what you are spending. Eventually, the Transaction Log discussed in Chapter III will help. For now, make your best estimate. You can adjust the numbers as your plan starts to work for you.

- ☐ Food. _____
- ☐ Periodic payment account
  (see Chapter V). _____

- ☐ Clothing. _____
- ☐ Medical expenses. _____
- ☐ Auto repairs. _____
- ☐ Home repairs. _____
- ☐ Emergency repair account (see Chapter V). _____
- ☐ Personal expenses. _____
- ☐ Family members' allowances. _____
- ☐ Gas for cars. _____
- ☐ Recreation. _____
- ☐ Subscriptions and books. _____
- ☐ Dues/membership fees. _____
- ☐ Gifts (birthdays, holidays). _____
- ☐ Contributions. _____
- ☐ Vacations. _____
- ☐ Child care. _____
- ☐ Tuition/education. _____
- ☐ Lessons. _____
- ☐ Hobbies. _____
- ☐ Auto registration/licenses. _____
- ☐ Dry cleaning and laundry. _____
- ☐ House cleaning. _____
- ☐ Newsstand purchases. _____
- ☐ Home improvements. _____
- ☐ Home furnishings. _____
- ☐ Emergency replacement account (see Chapter V). _____
- ☐ Pet care. _____

☐ _____   _____

☐ _____   _____

☐ _____   _____

You can, no doubt, think of additional expenses. List only those that apply to you.

You may have noticed that the expenses are organized into five groups. The first four (Taxes, Goals, Debts, and Contracts) are referred to as "fixed," since you have little or no control over the amount you spend each month. You may argue that goals are not really fixed, but you will be more successful in funding them if you treat them as if they are.

The fifth category, Day-to-Day, is known as "variable" because you have more control over these expenses.

As you complete your budget, pay careful attention to each of these five areas.

ADDING UP THE NUMBERS

Balancing your budget is one of the more difficult tasks that you will complete. But you can do it. Turn on your calculator and refer to your budget on page 26 to get started.

1. Total all Sources of Cash and record the amount on the line titled Total Cash Available.
2. Total all Uses of Cash and record the amount on the line titled Total Cash to Be Spent.
3. Subtract the amount of the Total Cash to Be Spent from the amount of Total Cash Available. Put your number on the line titled Surplus (or Deficit). If the number is negative, put parentheses around it.

If the number is positive, you have a surplus. Your expenditures are less than your income. However, before you start celebrating, ask yourself:

YOUR BUDGET

From _____ (month and year) to _____ (month and year)

Sources of Cash	Annual Targets	Monthly Targets
1 _____	_____	_____
2 _____	_____	_____
3 _____	_____	_____
4 _____	_____	_____
5 _____	_____	_____
6 _____	_____	_____
Total Cash Available:	_____	1524.25

Uses of Cash

	Annual Targets	Monthly Targets
1 _____	_____	_____
2 _____	_____	_____
3 _____	_____	_____
4 _____	_____	_____
5 _____	_____	_____
6 _____	_____	_____
7 _____	_____	_____
8 _____	_____	_____
9 _____	_____	_____
10 _____	_____	_____
11 _____	_____	_____
12 _____	_____	_____
13 _____	_____	_____
14 _____	_____	_____
15 _____	_____	_____
16 _____	_____	_____
Total Cash to Be Spent:	_____	_____
Surplus (or Deficit):	_____	_____

- [ ] Did you leave out any expenditures?
- [ ] Are any expenditure estimates too low?
- [ ] Did you punch in all numbers accurately on your calculator? Compare the tape to the figures in the Annual Targets column.

If the number is negative, you have a deficit. Your expenditures are larger than your income, and you have some work to do. Don't be discouraged. Nine times out of ten the number is negative at this point in the process.

MAKING THE NUMBERS WORK

If your budget is out of line, you have two basic choices. You can reduce your spending or increase your income. Let's take a look at different ways you can accomplish each.

Reduce expenditures

Balancing a budget is often difficult because you may make spending decisions in terms of gross income. Yet a large percentage of your expenditures may be fixed and not adjustable.

You may need to lower your expectations in certain areas. Starting with your day-to-day expenses, take each one at a time and ask, Can this expense be reduced, postponed, or eliminated?

As you consider ways to cut expenses without dramatically affecting your lifestyle, keep the following simple strategies in mind.

Make lists. Lists are essential when grocery shopping and are recommended anytime you shop. You are less likely to buy on impulse when shopping with a list. A list identifies what you want to buy, and keeps you from forgetting why you went shopping in the first place.

Tip: Never go grocery shopping when you are hungry. Everything looks good and studies show hungry shoppers spend more money.

Real life, real answers.

Peggy and David Silver's expected expenses exceeded their projected income by $2,400 the first time they tried budgeting. They sat down with their two children to see what expenditures they could reduce, postpone, or eliminate. The item with the lowest priority in their budget was "subscriptions." Their decision not to renew one newspaper and two magazines saved them $132. Their decision to defer until next year redecorating the master bedroom saved an additional $1,400. After reducing three other expenses by $868, they were able to balance their budget without having to sacrifice too much or feel they were scrimping.

Take cash when shopping. When buying food, clothing, or gifts, use cash instead of checks or credit cards. This is an effective way to limit impulse buying.

Use coupons. You can find coupons for almost anything. Not only are they good at the grocery store, but coupons are available for service stations, restaurants (two dinners for the price for one), and the theater, for example.

Watch for sales. Learn to buy clothing at the end of the season, when prices have been dramatically reduced. Plan your spending so that you can wait for sales to make major purchases, including appliances.

Give up or cut back on a money-burning habit such as smoking. If smoking costs you $1 a day and you put that money instead into a money market account paying 7 percent interest, at the end of 40 years you would have more than $75,000. What's more, your odds of living that long would vastly improve.

Take your lunch to work. Again, if you save just $1 a day, you are talking about a very hefty retirement nest egg after 30 or 40 years.

Take advantage of free or inexpensive recreational and educational opportunities in your community. After all, your tax dollars pay for the local library, state parks, and historical sights. Tuition at community educational classes is usually a great buy.

Think twice the next time you want to replace something. Ask yourself: Can I do without this item? Can it be repaired? Can I repair it? Can I get by renting the item instead of buying it?

Research a product or service before you buy. Your local librarian can help.

Complain effectively when a product or service is defective. If the local merchant will not make adjustments, develop the habit of writing to the president of the firm that makes the product or offers the service. Explain why you were not satisfied, and what happened when you returned to the store and asked for an adjustment. The president of the firm cares more about satisfied customers than do most store clerks.

Look into saving money on insurance. Prices vary for the same types of coverage. Periodically check to see if you can get identical coverage for less. But never cancel any policy until the new one is in force.

Simon Leeds was tired of writing fat checks for automobile insurance. He called his agent to investigate the possibility of reducing his premium. His agent informed him that by taking a driver's education course, Simon would save $150 annually on insurance. Simon registered for the course and is a better driver to boot.

Look at deductibles on your insurance policies. A higher deductible translates into lower premium payments.

Put everyone in the family on an allowance. Give each person enough money at the beginning of the week for things like gas, lunches, and personal grooming. Agree that how anyone spends his or her allowance is not subject to audit by any other family member.

If tempted to buy it on credit, compare the "cash" price with the "charge it" price.

Buy secondhand. It is invariably much cheaper.

Tip: Run a "want to buy" ad in the classified section of your paper or check for local yard sales before buying an item new in the stores. Children's bicycles and sporting equipment are examples of items you can find at reasonable prices if you buy secondhand.

Be car-conscious. Do you have a gas-guzzling car? Does your car find it hard to pass a repair shop? Maybe it is time to replace it. If you are not car-conscious, consult the latest April issue of *Consumer Reports*. It will help you select a car that fits your needs and that has an excellent repair record. Look for one that averages better than 30 miles per gallon. But before you buy, check with your insurance agent about car insurance premiums. They vary greatly from one make to the next.

Ask your family or friends for creative ways to reduce expenses.

Your total expenditures must never exceed your income. In rare instances, you will be unable to reduce expenditures enough. When this happens, you must increase your income.

Increase income

There are three reasons why people try to balance a budget by increasing income.

1. Their current income is not adequate to provide for their basic needs.

2. They owe too much money to too many creditors. While there are a variety of explanations for this, generally credit has been used to satisfy wants rather than to meet basic needs. People who have serious credit problems usually have difficulty distinguishing between wants and needs.

3. They fail to plan for major financial needs that will inevitably occur in the future. Doing without today so funds will be available for future obligations is not easy.

If one spouse is unemployed, a part-time or full-time job may be just the ticket needed to increase income. But before adding

Real life, real answers.

G inny and Fred Quinn had decided that Ginny would stay at home when their son was born, but after six months it became clear that Fred's $33,000 salary was not enough. So Ginny went back to work.

Eight months later, they were frustrated. Ginny's income of $22,000 didn't seem to be helping very much. They sat down to analyze just where her salary was going.

Child care	$ 5,000
Income taxes	6,300
Social Security	1,700
Lunches out	600
Clothing	1,000
Personal care	400
Second car	3,000
Dinners out	1,800
Total expenses	$19,800
Surplus	$ 2,200

The Quinns felt they could make changes in two areas: dinners out and the second car.

Restaurants and takeout food had become especially convenient since Ginny had returned to work. The couple decided to change their approach to mealtimes. By cooking more at home and making use of convenience foods, they cut their restaurant bills in half—to $900.

The second car had seemed necessary at the time they bought it. Ginny's carpool could not accommodate dropping off the baby at the day-care center near her office. Now she and Fred did some research and found a day-care center close to Fred's office. That center was $500 cheaper and they saved another $2,700 by selling the car. An added bonus—Fred is enjoying the extra time with his son.

Ginny and Fred found their savings strategies relatively painless to implement. A year later Ginny received a substantial raise and promotion, making them even happier with their decision.

a second breadwinner to the family, make sure that enough money will be left after subtracting additional costs such as clothing, lunches, transportation, child care, and taxes (state and federal income taxes and Social Security). There are many other good reasons for working aside from income, but make sure a second income is actually cost-effective.

You also may be able to increase your income by lowering your taxes. Recent changes in the tax laws have reduced the number of shelters and deductions for which you once may have qualified. But the two best shelters are still owning a home and funding retirement.

Home ownership. The interest on the mortgage and the property taxes you pay qualify as itemized deductions. They will reduce your taxable income dollar for dollar if you can itemize.

Funding retirement. Income put into a 401(k) at work will reduce your taxable income dollar for dollar. You may also qualify for an IRA; most people still do. If self-employed, you may want to consider setting up a Keogh plan or SEP. But be sure your budget can handle the contribution. File a new W-4 at work if you receive a large federal income tax refund each spring.

> **Tip:** Never under withhold, as the IRS will charge you interest on the shortage, plus a fine if your withholding is not at least 90 percent of your federal tax liability.

LAST RESORT

If you are unable to balance your budget by either reducing expenditures or increasing income, there are a few more options to contemplate: restructuring your debt load, adjusting your goals, and using credit.

Restructure your debts

Shop around for lower interest rates on charge accounts.You may want to consolidate all your debts using a home equity line

Real life, real answers.

A fter renting an apartment for several years, Lynne Ziskin is considering buying a $60,000 condo. She plans to make a $10,000 down payment and figures that she can get a fixed 30-year mortgage with an interest rate of 10 percent.

Lynne's rent over a five-year period totals $41,000. Assuming that she will sell the condo in five years, Lynne makes the following "rent vs. buy" estimate.

Costs

Closing costs, points, (a point is 1 percent of your mortgage), and loan origination fees	$ 3,000
Repairs and maintenance contract	7,000
Property taxes	3,000
Mortgage payments	26,000
Sales commission, closing costs (when selling)	7,000
Total Ownership Costs	$46,000

Benefits

Reduction in mortgage loan	$2,000
Tax savings deducting interest and property taxes	7,000
Gross profit (when selling)	15,000
Total Ownership Benefits	$24,000
Actual cost of owning a condo	$22,000

Lynne figures she is better off by $19,000 if she buys the condo. However, an accountant friend points out to her that a key in her equation is the assumption of profit Lynne expects to realize when she resells the condo after five years. Because the increase in housing prices has slowed in many areas, Lynne will be fortunate if she makes her $15,000 profit. Her friend also points out that the $10,000 she plans on using for the down payment will earn interest over that same five-year period. Lynne still feels she will be better off buying the condo than continuing to rent.

of credit. Your interest rate will be lower than any rates charged by a credit card company, and your interest will be tax deductible. (In 1990, only 10 percent of the interest paid on consumer loans and credit cards is deductible; starting in 1991, none of it is.) Because applying for a home equity line of credit can cost several hundred dollars, take the time to find the best deal.

Home equity lines of credit can be misused because you can so easily borrow against them by writing a check. Use them for consolidating your debts only. You are risking your home if you abuse this line of credit.

Adjust your goals

Reduce or eliminate funding for a particularly expensive goal. Don't worry. You will probably be able to restore the goal soon. Next time you get a pay raise, use some of it to fund it. Once you have made the last payment to a creditor, begin depositing the same amount into a savings account.

Use credit

If you are still unable to balance income and expenditures, you are going to have to borrow. This should be a last resort, but it may be your only option. The time should soon come when you will rarely if ever have to borrow if you carefully develop and follow your budget.

Now that your spending plan has been developed, it is time to see it in action. You've done some of the hardest work already. You know what your goals are. You've answered some difficult questions and have worked out a budget. It's time to put your budget into play.

CHAPTER III

Your spending plan in action

Y ou now know how you want to spend your money. You may feel you have accomplished what you set out to do by developing a budget. But now you must follow that budget and put your spending plan to work.

Let your budget guide you. But first make sure your recordkeeping and bill-paying methods are as efficient as possible.

CHOOSING THE BEST BANKING SERVICES

Let's start with your checking account. Banks offer a dazzling variety of checking accounts and services.

Can your checking account pass this test? (Answer each question yes or no.)

_____ 1. Do you earn interest on all funds in your account from the day money is deposited until the day money is withdrawn? Usually such accounts pay 5 to 5½ percent. Most banks will require a minimum balance between $500 to $1,000, but look at what you get in exchange:

☐ You pay no monthly service charge.
☐ The bank pays you interest on the required minimum balance.
☐ The bank pays you interest on other money in the account as long as it remains there.

With what you save in service charges plus the interest you earn on the minimum deposit, you are already saving money.

_____ **2.** Does the account come with a credit or debit card? A debit card looks like a credit card, but purchases made with them are handled as if they were made with checks.

_____ **3.** Is overdraft protection available on the account? There may be times when you inadvertently overdraw your checking account. With overdraft protection you will not be fined by the bank. Such protection can be a mixed blessing because it makes it easy to "borrow" money. If you are currently having problems managing your credit, overdraft protection may not be for you at this time.

_____ **4.** Do you have access to automated teller machines (ATMs)? This is a nice convenience if you make deposits or withdrawals after banking hours or if you do not like standing in lines.

_____ **5.** Does the bank return your canceled checks? Although many banks send you only a list of your checks, the actual check is preferable for tax purposes.

_____ **6.** Does the bank list your checks in number sequence on statements? This simple convenience makes it easier when you reconcile your check stubs with the bank statement.

_____ **7.** Is the bank willing to automatically transfer funds to pay your contractual expenses? Can your checking account make automatic payments to an insurance company or mutual fund?

You should be able to answer yes to all seven questions. If you cannot, open a new account with a bank that will provide these services.

SETTING UP YOUR ACCOUNTS AND IMPROVING SERVICES

A successful spending plan may require more than one checking account. If you are married or living with someone, each partner might have his or her own checking account. Consider dividing up expenses so each partner is responsible for certain ones. Accounts will be easier to manage if you each have one and keep separate records.

You will manage your money more efficiently if some of your payments are handled automatically. How many of the following automatic transfers are you already using?

1. If there is a 401(k) savings plan at work, do you have part of your paycheck deposited into the 401(k) account? If you are currently participating in such a plan, you should be familiar with the following benefits:

☐ Your taxable income for the year is reduced by every dollar deposited into the 401(k).

☐ The income earned on the money you deposit into the 401(k) plan is not taxed until you withdraw it upon retirement.

☐ Most employers offer a matching program. For example, if 6 percent of your salary is deposited into the 401(k), your employer might put in an additional 3 percent.

2. Can you have money withheld at work to buy government Series EE Savings Bonds? Interest income on Series EE Bonds bought after January 1, 1990, is not taxed if the money is used to pay for a college education. If you are now trying to save money to earn a degree several years in the future, consider purchasing Series EE Savings Bonds through a payroll savings plan at work.

3. Is your paycheck automatically deposited to your checking account?

4. Have you asked your bank to automatically transfer a regular monthly amount of money from your checking account to a savings or money market account to fund your goals?

5. If you are trying to save for long-term goals, have you given a mutual fund permission to withdraw a specific dollar amount from your checking account on a regular basis?

6. Have you asked your bank to automatically make payments such as your mortgage and car loans?

7. Have you given your life insurance company permission to withdraw the amount of your premium payment?

8. If you are on a budget plan with your utility company, can they bill your account each month?

You may identify other automatic transfer services such as telephone transfers. Be sure to record each transfer.

Automatic transfers are beneficial because you save time and postage and you avoid late charges and penalties. You therefore will be more successful at funding your goals.

KEEPING A TRANSACTION LOG

A Transaction Log is a simple recordkeeping system that lets you know at any time how much money you have left to spend before your next payday.

A TRANSACTION LOG

				BE SURE TO DEDUCT CHARGES THAT AFFECT YOUR ACCOUNT			
Date	Check number	Description of transaction		SUBTRACTIONS		ADDITIONS	BALANCE FORWARD
				Amount of Payment	4	TAX	Amount of Deposit	

The log is similar to that of a check register, so if you've always kept an accurate account in your checkbook, you will be on familiar ground here. The Transaction Log will simply replace your old system. If you've been using your check register for a scratch pad, the Transaction Log is for you.

As with a check register, each check you write and each cash withdrawal you make is recorded in the Transaction Log along with your deposits. But, because you will also write down individual credit card purchases, the log will more accurately reflect your cash flow (your expenditures and your income).

Filling in the Transaction Log

As you can see from the sample, the log is just a checkbook register. (You can pick up a new register at your bank.) It consists of columns for the date, the check number or transaction code, the description of the transaction, the amount of the deposit or withdrawal, and the balance. Filling in your Transaction Log is simple. Let's take a look at each type of transaction.

Deposits. Each deposit is recorded in the Transaction Log. You need to include:

1. The date of the deposit (usually deposits made at banks after 2 p.m. will be credited to your account the following business day).

2. A description of the transaction; that is, whether it was a paycheck, dividend, tax refund, Social Security payment, etc.

3. The dollar amount. Don't forget to add the deposit to the balance.

4. A "D" in the code column.

Checks. You need to include:

1. The date of the check.

2. A description of the transaction (the person or company to whom the check was made payable).

3. The dollar amount; remember to subtract the amount of the check from the balance.

4. The number of the check in the code column.

5. A note as to whether this expenditure has income tax consequences (by placing a "T" in the code column).

Debit cards. If you use debit cards, record them as you would a check with one difference: Put "DC" in the code column instead of a check number. Subtract from the balance.

Cash withdrawals. Cash withdrawals are recorded like checks, but put a "CW" in the code column. Subtract from the balance.

Bank charges. Record bank charges that appear on your monthly statement (such as service, check printing, or overdraft charges) as you would record a check, but put a "B" in the code column. Subtract from the balance.

Automatic transfers. Automatic transfers should be logged in as you would enter a check, but use "AT" in the code column. Subtract from the balance.

Tip: Use automatic transfers to make loan payments; purchase mutual fund shares; pay insurance premiums; pay utility bills (if you are on a budget plan); fund goals; fund your other accounts.

Credit card purchases. These are recorded as you would record a check with two differences. After you have recorded the amount of the charge, circle the dollar amount. And don't put anything in the code column yet. Subtract the amount of the purchase from the balance. When you do write the check to the credit card company, you will then go back and insert the check number next to each item that appeared on the credit card statement.

Take a look at a sample page from Mary Wilson's Transaction Log on page 41. There are five credit card charges circled, but only the first three appear on her March bill, as shown on page 42. And since Mary's first goal is to eliminate the debt she owes the credit card company, she wants to send enough money to pay off the current month's interest plus a part of the

MARY WILSON'S TRANSACTION LOG

BE SURE TO DEDUCT CHARGES THAT AFFECT YOUR ACCOUNT

Date	Check number	Description of transaction	Amount of Payment	4	TAX	Amount of Deposit	BALANCE FORWARD
							946
3/19	AT	Car payment	280 —				666
3/18	590	Clothing	(90) —				576
3/19	577	Food	129 —				447
3/20	578	Gift to Charlie	32 —				415
3/20	579	Education loan	67 —				348
3/21	580	Cash	20 —				328
3/22	590	Health club	(38) —				290
3/23	590	Car repair	(51) —				239
3/28	581	Water bill	45 —				194
3/29	582	club dues	55 —				139
3/31	D	payroll				1150 —	1289
3/31	B	safety deposit box	25				1264
4/1	583	Rent	750				514
4/2	D	Modeling				90	604
4/2	CW	Cash	50				554
4/6	AT	Life insurance	45				509
4/7	584	phone bill	36				473
4/8	585	Night school tuition	279				194
4/13	AT	Fidelity Mutual Fund	100				94
4/13	D	Payroll				1150 —	1244
4/14		Clothing	(52)				1192
4/15	586	Food	104				1088
4/15	AT	Periodic payment account	215				873
4/15	587	natural gas bill	65				808
4/15	588	paper subscription	30				778
4/15	589	dentist	225				553
4/16		Clothing	(24)				529
4/19	D	Modeling				180	709
4/14	B	new checks	10				699
4/17	B	interest earned				10	709
4/18	590	Credit card interest	35				674
4/18	590	Credit card balance payments	50				624

Transaction Log Codes:
"D" - deposit
"#" - checks
"DC" - debit card

"CW" - cash withdrawal
"T" - item has tax consequences
"B" - bank charges
"AT" - automatic transfer

41

MARY WILSON'S CREDIT CARD ACCOUNT STATEMENT

STATEMENT CLOSING DATE: MARCH, 1990

Account number: 987654321
Mary Wilson
Quimby Court
Anywhere, USA 10001

Send payment to:
Bank Card
P.O. Box 555
Creditville, USA 20001

Previous balance:	$2,300.00	Interest:	$35.00
Payments:	$300.00	Balance due:	$2,214.00
New charges:	$179.00	Minimum payment:	$105.00

3/18	Crystal's Fashion	$90.00
3/22	Power Health Club	$38.00
3/23	Acme Auto Repair	$51.00
Total charges for the month:		$179.00

---

unpaid balance from last month. The amount of her check number 590 is broken down as follows:

☐ $179 for three purchases listed on this month's statement
☐ $35 for the interest for the month (entered in Log)
☐ $50 toward the previous month's balance (entered in her Log)

The total amount of the check she writes is $264.

Tip: Bookkeeping will be easier if you use a single credit card for your personal expenses.

Recording checks and charges in a Transaction Log gives you excellent documentation of where you spend your money. Record purchases as you make them and keep the balance current. You will always know precisely how much you have. Remember to add deposits and subtract checks, debit card purchases, credit card charges, cash withdrawals, and automatic transfers from the balance.

If you and your spouse or partner have separate accounts, you must keep separate Transaction Logs. If you maintain different checking accounts for different purposes, each of these will require a log as well.

You now have a clear record of your spending. In the next chapter, we will monitor how you are doing.

CHAPTER IV

How are you doing?

It's time to balance your books and compare your actual spending with your budget. You will now reconcile your Transaction Log with your bank and credit card statements.

If the numbers are not meshing as well as you had hoped, don't be too hard on yourself. Old habits do die hard. Following a budget takes discipline and commitment. Give yourself time. Although you should already notice improvements in the way you manage your money, it will be a while before you feel totally in control and at ease. But don't you feel better about your overall financial situation? You should. Like embarking on a successful diet or exercise regimen, you have admitted to yourself that you want to change and have decided to do something about it. And you've taken the first steps.

As you read this section, take note of what is working for you and what isn't.

CHECKING YOUR TRANSACTION LOG AGAINST YOUR STATEMENTS

Your checking account must be reconciled with the monthly bank statement.

Tip: As with credit card statements, always check your records against your bank statements. Mistakes are inadvertent but they do occur. It is your job as a money manager to double check the numbers.

RECONCILING YOUR TRANSACTION LOG WITH YOUR BANK STATEMENT

Reconciliation Statement for (month _____ / year _____)

1. End balance on bank statement. $ _____

2. Bank deposits made after closing
    date of statement.   _____

                                              _____

                                              _____

                                              _____

                                                       $ _____

3. Add amounts on lines one and two.   _____

4. Subtract all checks and credit card
    purchases that have not cleared your
    checking account (those that are not
    listed on your statement).   _____

                                              _____

                                              _____

                                              _____

                                              _____

                                              _____

                                              _____

                                              _____

                                              _____

                                              _____

                                              _____

                                                       $ _____

5. Balance in Transaction Log.   _____

   (A similar reconciliation form appears on the back of your bank statement.)

To make sure that your records agree with those of your bank, complete the following steps. You've probably been following this procedure for years, but if you've been a bit lax, the detailed instructions that follow will be helpful.

1. Make sure each deposit listed in your Transaction Log is also listed on your bank statement. Put a checkmark in the column to the left of each deposit listed in the log. Also, put a checkmark next to the same deposit listed on the bank statement. Are there any deposits listed in your Transaction Log that are not listed in your bank statement? If you have made deposits to your checking account after the date of the bank statement, list the total amount for these deposits on line 2 of the Reconciliation Statement.

If a deposit does not appear on your bank statement, check to make sure it was made during the period covered by the statement. If there is a discrepancy, take a copy of your deposit receipt to a bank officer and ask to be credited for the missing deposit. (Have any interest due added on if it is an interest-earning account.)

Tip: Always hold on to deposit receipts. When you take issue with your bank's accounting, always bring in or send copies of your records. Keep originals in your possession.

If the bank has made a mistake and bounced a check, insist that the bank write a letter of explanation to the creditor. Keep your credit rating clean.

If you failed to record any deposits in your Transaction Log, add them now and adjust the balance accordingly.

2. Match all the checks listed in your bank statement against all the checks listed in your Transaction Log. Most statements list checks in number sequence; this is extremely helpful. In the column to the right of the Amount of Payment column in the log, put checkmarks next to each check listed on the statement. Re-

member that the check number written to a credit card company may be listed in more than one place in your log depending on how many charges you made during a given month. When these are added together, they should equal the total amount of the check.

3. Using your calculator, total the amount of all the checks you have written that are not listed on the bank statement.

4. You may also have bank transactions such as the following listed on your statement:

☐ Check printing charges.
☐ Check processing and transaction fees.
☐ Monthly service charge.
☐ Monthly interest earned.
☐ Safety deposit box rental fee.

As you identify each bank transaction listed on your bank statement, make sure each has been recorded and checkmarked in the Transaction Log. Remember to subtract the amount from the balance.

5. Now it is time to examine the debit card purchases and automatic transfers. Handle them like checks. Check off each debit card and automatic transfer on the bank statement and the Transaction Log. If debit card purchases and automatic transfers are listed on the bank statement, but not listed in the Transaction log, record each unentered transaction in your log and adjust the balance.

6. Record the final balance on the bank statement on line 1 of the Reconciliation Statement.

7. Add the amount on line 2 (deposits made after the closing date) to the final balance on line 1 and record it on line 3.

8. Subtract the amount on line 4 (outstanding checks and credit card purchases) from the total on line 3 and record it on line 5. The resulting number should be identical to the balance in your Transaction Log. If it is, draw a box around the balance in your log. That box tells you that you have reconciled the bank

statement with the balance in your Transaction Log.

If the number on line 5 does not agree with the balance in the Transaction Log, check each entry on the Reconciliation Statement. First make sure you copied each number accurately. Then check the calculator tape that lists all outstanding checks by running a new tape.

You may have made a mathematical error when making entries in the Transaction Log. Go back to the last boxed balance in the log. Add and subtract every entry starting with the balance in the box to make sure that the present balance in the Transaction Log is accurate.

If the number on line 5 is larger than the balance in your Transaction Log, make sure you subtracted all outstanding checks. Did you go back far enough? Could there be a check written four or five months ago that never cleared your account?

If the number on line 5 is smaller than the balance in your Transaction Log, you may be missing a deposit somewhere. Start again at step 1 to find the problem, and stay with it until you have balanced the bank statement with the Transaction Log.

Repeat this process for each checking and money market account. When all accounts are in balance, you are ready to find out how your actual spending matches up with your planned spending.

SPENDING CONTROL SHEET

How well does actual spending compare with planned spending? To answer this question, you need to complete the Spending Control Sheet on page 50. (You may need to do a Spending Control Sheet for only a few months to get back on track; then use it as the need arises.)

The first column lists your income and expense categories just as they appear in your budget. The second column lists your budget estimates (or targets) for each income and expenditure category. The third column contains actual numbers. Expendi-

SPENDING CONTROL SHEET

(Month and Year)

Sources of Cash	Monthly Targets	Actual Expenses	Variance
1 _____	_____	_____	_____
2 _____	_____	_____	_____
3 _____	_____	_____	_____
4 _____	_____	_____	_____
5 _____	_____	_____	_____
6 _____	_____	_____	_____

Total Cash Available:

Uses of Cash

	Monthly Targets	Actual Expenses	Variance
1 _____	_____	_____	_____
2 _____	_____	_____	_____
3 _____	_____	_____	_____
4 _____	_____	_____	_____
5 _____	_____	_____	_____
6 _____	_____	_____	_____
7 _____	_____	_____	_____
8 _____	_____	_____	_____
9 _____	_____	_____	_____
10 _____	_____	_____	_____
11 _____	_____	_____	_____
12 _____	_____	_____	_____
13 _____	_____	_____	_____
14 _____	_____	_____	_____
15 _____	_____	_____	_____
16 _____	_____	_____	_____

Total Cash to Be Spent: _____ _____ _____

Surplus (or Deficit): _____ _____ _____

tures paid by check will be easier to record than day-to-day expenses because you often pay cash for those items. If you have been keeping a diary for cash expenses, you are ahead of the game.

Complete the Spending Control Sheet by working through these steps.

1. List all income and expense categories just as they are listed in column 1 of your budget.

2. In the Monthly Targets column, record each monthly expense exactly as it appears under the same column heading in your budget.

3. Start to fill in the blanks in column 3, Actual Expenses. The first income category in your budget is probably your salary. You are going to need your pay stub. It indicates the gross amount of your paycheck before money is withheld for income taxes, Social Security, and so forth. Record your gross salary or wages. Next record federal and state income taxes, Social Security, and any other payroll deductions (contribution to a 401(k), for example) under Uses of Cash in column 3. Check to make sure that the net amount of your paycheck is the same as the deposit recorded in your Transaction Log.

4. Refer back to your Transaction Log. Begin with the next income source listed in your budget. Once you have accounted for all sources of income recorded in your log, you are ready to begin recording expenditures. To keep from counting a transaction more than once, put a checkmark next to it in the log as you record it on the Spending Control Sheet.

5. During the budgeting period you probably withdrew cash several times. That cash was probably used to make a variety of purchases. If you have not been keeping a diary, you will only be able to guess how you spent it. But estimate as accurately as you can. Continue this process until all expenditures recorded in the Transaction Log have been listed in column 3 of the Spending Control Sheet.

How did you do?

You are now ready to see how well you did. Starting with the first category in the Spending Control Sheet, subtract the actual amount in column 3 from the planned or targeted amount in column 2. Record the result in column 4, Variance. (These numbers are known as "variances" because each number indicates how actual spending varied from planned spending.) When the number is negative (the amount in column 3 is larger than the amount in column 2), put brackets around the number.

Circle the three or four expenditures that show the largest negative variance (the highest negative numbers in column 4). These expenditures need a tighter rein.

To better control these unruly numbers, ask yourself, Was the original planned estimate for the expense too low?

Tip: Keep targets realistic. Don't saddle the person who is responsible for a certain expense with an impossible task.

Be careful. If you increase the spending target for one expense, you must reduce the target for another to maintain the structural integrity of the budget.

☐ Are your expenses high because your insurance coverage is inadequate? You may need to reevaluate your coverage if this is a problem.

☐ Is the person responsible for a runaway expense monitoring it properly? If the expense is significantly over target, it is not being watched as closely as it should be. Keep a minilog for a month as an exercise in keeping spending in this category under control.

☐ Have you been able to fund the goals listed in your budget? If this is a stumbling block, keep in mind that automatic transfers make goal funding easier.

☐ Are you making payments to creditors on time? Chapters VII and VIII will help you in this area.

Don't get frustrated if several expenses exceed your spending target. This is normal. Your budget must have some elasticity. Look for an expenditure that is under target and juggle the numbers to make the balance click.

Making adjustments in your budget will be an ongoing process. Remember that your budget is helping you accomplish three very important goals: paying off your debt, saving for future needs, and living comfortably today. Give it (and yourself) time.

CHAPTER V

Traps and tips

B udgeting is not an exact science. It requires field testing and adjustments. Ideally, you will ultimately "goof proof" your budget so the time and effort you put into developing a spending plan pays you back.

Following are a few examples of potential villains lurking in the dark corners of your budget.

MEDICAL AND REPAIR ACCOUNT

Glitch one: A large medical bill or repair bill comes in unexpectedly and your budget is wrecked. You may be forced to resort to using credit in order to cover your expenses.

Solution: Most budgets are not set up to handle repairs adequately. You will need to refer to your records (checkbooks, bills, and charge account statements) to complete the form on page 56. You need to know what you paid in repair and medical bills for the past 12 months. For the medical, dental, and optometrist bills, fill in the amount you actually paid.

Use the total amount when working this cushion into your budget. You may need to adjust the amount (either up or down) if your experience for the past 12 months was atypical.

To find out what your monthly medical and repair expenses will be, simply divide the number by 12.

The Nields family determined that they spent, on an average, $150 a month on medical and repair bills. They budgeted

REPAIR AND MEDICAL BILLS

EXPENSE	ANNUAL TOTAL
Auto repairs	$ _____
Home repairs	_____
Appliance repairs	_____
Medical bills (and prescriptions)	_____
Optometrist (and eyewear)/dental bills	_____
Other	_____
Total	$ _____

that amount every month. If, however, they did not need that much in a given month, they placed the extra funds in a special account. That way, when a larger expense came in, they were prepared.

You might consider two refinements on the Nields family's technique.

1. Have your bank transfer funds to the medical/repair account automatically. You will not be tempted to dip into those funds on those months when such bills are small.

2. Place the budgeted funds in a money market account. You can then write checks as needed. Money market accounts earn a higher rate of interest than standard savings or checking accounts.

How much money should you keep in this account? That depends on your situation. Are you likely to be laid off? Does your income vary from month to month? This is an emergency fund. The less stable your income, the heftier the balance you should maintain.

Tip: Remember what this account is for: medical and repair bills. Do not rob it to buy a new appliance or use it to pay off a debt.

If you do not have a medical/repair account, set one up now. Factor the amount you will need each month into your budget. Setting up this single account can do more to sustain your budget than getting the raise you've been hankering for.

PERIODIC PAYMENT ACCOUNT

Glitch two: You did not budget enough money for periodic expenses such as insurance premiums, car licenses and registration fees, property taxes, gifts, tuition, and vacations. These expenses, if overlooked, can do as much damage to your budget as an unexpected medical bill.

Solution: These expenditures are easier to control than unexpected expenses because you know when they are coming and you can estimate the dollar amount of each expense. Periodic expenses require the same approach as the medical and repair account.

PERIODIC PAYMENTS

EXPENSE	ANNUAL AMOUNT
Auto insurance	$ _____
Homeowners insurance	_____
Life insurance	_____
Property taxes	_____
Auto licenses	_____
Gifts	_____
Birthdays	_____
Vacations	_____
College tuition	_____
School expenses	_____
Other	_____
Total	$ _____

Divide your total (a reflection of your expected annual expenses) by 12 and have your bank automatically transfer the money into a separate account, such as a money market account. This will guarantee that you will have the funds when you need them. But resist spending the money you have budgeted for periodic expenses if there are no such expenses in a particular month.

You should expect to maintain a minimum balance of at least $1,000—more if you can swing it.

REPLACEMENT ACCOUNT

Glitch three: Your sofa is threadbare and your 12-year-old washing machine is making odd noises. Will you have enough money to purchase replacements without having to use credit?

Solution: Set up a replacement account along the lines of your repair/medical account and your periodic payment account. You may go for months or years without needing to replace a major item and then, in a matter of two weeks, need to make several large purchases.

To figure out how much you will need, fill in the blanks on the following form. A sample has been completed for you.

Item	Life Expectancy	Current Age	Life Left	Cost	Annual Savings Required
Washer	12 years	8 years	4 years	$400	$100
Dryer	15 years	_____	_____	_____	_____
Car	10 years	_____	_____	_____	_____
Refrigerator	16 years	_____	_____	_____	_____
Stove	18 years	_____	_____	_____	_____
Microwave	10 years	_____	_____	_____	_____
TV	15 years	_____	_____	_____	_____
_____	_____	_____	_____	_____	_____
_____	_____	_____	_____	_____	_____

Total Annual Replacement Savings Needed $_____

To complete this form:

☐ Subtract "Current Age" for each item from "Life Expectancy." This gives you an estimate of "Life Left" or remaining years of service.

☐ Divide "Life Left" into the current cost for each item to figure out the annual savings required so you can pay cash when you replace an item.

☐ Add all "Annual Savings" to give you the total.

Your replacement expenses can be handled in the same way as repairs and periodic payments. Most people don't include an account in their budgets for replacing items as they wear out, so this replacement account could be a new expense for you.

You may not agree with the life expectancy of certain items listed on the chart. For instance, you might want to trade in your car more often than once a decade, or buy a television more frequently than the chart indicates. If you reduce the life expectancy of an item because of your own lifestyle, make sure the resulting higher numbers are shown in your calculations.

Right now you may not have enough money to adequately fund the replacement account. Your actual monthly deposit may be significantly less than the computed monthly deposit you arrived at by dividing the Total Annual Replacement Savings by 12. Don't worry. You can increase the monthly deposit when you get a raise, or when you pay off a creditor.

If you have the self-discipline not to dip into the funds you have budgeted for medical expenses, repair bills, periodic payments, and replacement costs, you might not need these extra accounts. That's fine; you'll save some money on annual fees and service charges. But if you are tempted, keep your money in separate accounts. You may find that one account can handle these expenses. Don't be afraid to experiment. Do what works best for you.

UTILITY BILLING PLAN

Glitch four: Your utility bills vary widely from month to month. Depending on the season and where you live, your winter bills and summer bills can be as different as an Alaskan winter from a Florida summer.

Solution: Contact your utility companies. Ask them to explain their budget plans. They can estimate a monthly average for you based on what you paid during the last 12 months. Utility companies know how much energy your household consumes each month. Once a year they will adjust your monthly payment up or down depending on rate changes and your consumption level.

These four glitches can trip anyone up. But you have been forewarned. The extra accounts (repair/medical, periodic payments, and replacement) will help keep your budget operating smoothly because they greatly reduce your need to borrow money.

CHAPTER VI

Budgets are family affairs

Money management is a family affair. You need to involve each member of your family in decisions about spending. As you fill in the charts sprinkled throughout this book, check to see whether your spouse or partner and/or children would have given similar responses. Their opinions are critical in making your budget work.

Give some thought to the following:

1. Who controls the money in your household? Is it one person? Is that working? If a spouse or partner is unhappy with the way the other partner dominates financial decisions, it is time for a family council. Encourage family members to be honest and speak up.

> **Tip:** If your spouse or partner holds the reins to the checkbooks and is secretive about family finances, insist on getting involved. Show you are interested and want to participate. Separations, divorces, disabilities, and deaths sadly do occur. When it comes to financial planning for the two of you, the last thing you want is an unpleasant surprise. If there is a problem that cannot be resolved between you, seek out professional counseling.

One partner might feel it is his or her duty to keep the family money situation private. That is unrealistic and unfair. Keeping a budget is a family responsibility. Share the load and strengthen the family bonds.

2. Your home is not a business. However, it is a training ground for helping children to become financially responsible adults. You might like to encourage a "hands-on" education. Let each teenage member of your family and the spouse or partner who does not regularly manage finances take a three-month turn at paying the bills. Each person will gain experience operating the budget and they will better understand where the money comes from and where it goes.

If one person makes all the family decisions, that person is cheating the rest of the family out of the opportunity of learning to handle money effectively.

Consider dividing expenses between you. Each partner will be solely responsible for certain expenses.

3. Does each member of your family have his or her own money to spend? It is essential that each family member has an allowance. It is their responsibility to make it last until "payday."

Everyone must be allowed to spend personal money, without fear of criticism or feelings of guilt. You should each work out a list of your needs to decide how much each family member should receive. Typically, such a list would include money for:

- ☐ Transportation expenses (gas, bus fare, tolls)
- ☐ Lunch
- ☐ Personal care (haircuts, manicures, dry cleaning)
- ☐ Gifts
- ☐ Clothing
- ☐ Magazines, books, and newspapers

Whether or not your children earn their allowances is up to you. Children should have chores for which they are not paid. They should be encouraged to perform some tasks on behalf of the family. However, consider "tipping" them for jobs such as yard work or washing the car.

Tip: Post "paying jobs" for your children on the refrigerator. Tailor different jobs to each child. Initiative should be rewarded.

4. When putting together the family budget, were the needs of each member considered? Before answering, mull over the following specifics:

☐ Have you decided on the level of financial support you plan to provide for each college-bound child? Have you discussed this with each child? Does he or she understand his or her part? In your current spending plan, are you saving and investing enough to meet your share?

☐ Aside from school and work, is money available for each member of the family to pursue a personal interest? Encourage your children to earn part of tuition or activity fees.

Tip: Try using a "matching program" with your children. If a child needs a specific sum for a special activity, agree to pay half of what is required. This way, your children will ask for matching funds only when they are serious about an activity and are willing to earn their share. Your children will feel good about themselves because they held up their end.

☐ Each member of your family should have input in selecting family recreational activities and vacations. Listen to their suggestions and preferences.

5. Do you use money to control your family members' behavior? Be careful. Withholding money as a punishment and doling out money as a reward is manipulation.

6. Are you giving your children ample opportunities to practice handling money responsibly? Just as each child needs to learn the relationship between work and compensation, each one needs to learn about spending and saving. Work with your children without being critical of their decisions. Help them develop their own budgets. You can work out a plan to help them

manage weekly allowances or help them with a long-range goal such as saving for a big purchase.

Tip: Younger children have a difficult time thinking beyond the next five minutes. Help them experience saving for a goal that can be realized in a week or two. Long-term goals become more realistic as the child gets older.

7. Do you and your spouse or partner maintain separate checking accounts? This practice makes money management plans run more efficiently and with less stress. Separate accounts keep your finances on a more even keel. You are less likely to disagree about specific purchases. It is also easier to balance a checking account when only one person has been using it. A personal account gives each partner something we all want and need: privacy.

8. Do you fight with your spouse or partner over money? Are your disagreements turning into arguments that are leading to a strained relationship?

Work through your disagreements by discussing them openly and frequently. Try to work as a team to achieve your individual and family financial goals. In some cases, an intermediary or professional counselor might be required. Do not be shy about getting help.

9. Does it seem like your partner spends money without thinking? Discuss the problem openly. Refrain from being critical, sarcastic, or confrontational. Money management experts agree that it is best to work together to decide how to spend your money and then split the responsibility for the expenditures. Each of you should manage part of the expenses. Together, you are responsible for managing the budget.

If one of you constantly exceeds the spending targets, reevaluate the targets. Are they realistic?

Your partner may simply not understand how the budget

works. Read this book together and discuss it. If your partner earns most or all of the family income, he or she may feel entitled to not have to worry about actually handling the money. But if your partner is a spendthrift, put him or her on a strict allowance. You may have to assume larger financial responsibilities. Do what works for you.

You and your partner might consider taking a course in basic money management skills. Check with your local community center or nearby college for a noncredit personal finance course. Think about taking the course together to facilitate easy, open communication.

If your partner's spending habits are really out of line, you may need to sit down with a professional intermediary. Impulsive, careless spending habits and shopping sprees may be a clue that something else is wrong. Periods of depression, low self-esteem, or lack of self-confidence may trigger a need to spend money. You may or may not know what is making your partner a "shopaholic." Whatever the cause, if you think you need the extra ear of a third party, get it.

CHAPTER VII

Using credit wisely

You know the problem. You scan your monthly credit card statement and ask yourself if you really spent that much. You weren't keeping track of each purchase, and they added up. The total amount due is a shock. It's more than your monthly income. But before reaching for an extra-strength antacid, you search for that little box with the comforting label, "minimum monthly payment required." Now there is a number you can handle. Before you can say "charge it," you are hooked on credit.

Does your paycheck seem to evaporate into thin air the moment you get it? Chances are your hard-earned dollars are being gobbled up by the Credit Monster.

Credit can be wonderful when used properly, but it is a terrible monster when misused. A heavy debt load is the primary reason why many individuals and families feel financially trapped, destined to live forever on the tightest of budgets.

Credit does make sense under certain conditions. Learn to use credit as it is used in the world of business. A bank or lending institution will not grant a business loan unless the proceeds will generate enough income to repay the loan. For example, a store wants to have more items to sell but the owner does not have the money to buy additional inventory. The owner shows the banker that a $10,000 loan will enable him or her to buy

$10,000 of new merchandise that can be sold for $20,000. Once the merchandise is sold, the $10,000 loan is repaid to the bank with interest. Such a model is the ideal approach for justifying a personal loan.

Unfortunately, most consumer loans do not fit this model. A consumer may borrow money to buy an item or service that is used up before it is paid for. The item or service purchased almost never generates the income to pay off the loan. There are, of course, exceptions to this rule.

☐ Money borrowed for an education usually results in the borrower qualifying for a higher-paying job. The student loan can be repaid out of the additional income.

☐ Money borrowed to buy a home can be a good investment, if you plan to live in the home five years or longer. Money previously used to pay rent makes most of the mortgage payment. The tax benefits from paying interest and property taxes usually make up the rest. When the house is sold, and the mortgage is paid off, the money left over is usually larger than the initial down payment.

☐ The monthly payments on a washer and dryer may be less than the cost of going to a laundromat (especially if you have children).

☐ A piano, for example, can pay for itself if someone in the family can earn enough giving piano lessons to make the monthly payments on it.

Keep in mind that even these "good" uses of credit can get you into trouble. For example, you can buy such an expensive home that your budget will be tight until the house is sold. The monthly payments required to repay a student loan can put a huge strain on your budget.

Can you take a businesslike approach to borrowing money? If you borrow only when the item or service you buy will generate the funds necessary to repay the loan, you have mastered credit. If you are in the habit of using credit every time the urge to buy something hits you, you may need to lock up your credit cards.

Use cash. If you start to pay cash for those things you previously bought on credit, you will benefit in several ways.

1. You will avoid interest expenses.
2. You will avoid late charges.
3. You will avoid loan application fees.
4. You may get a discount for cash.
5. You will think twice before spending.
6. You will not have to make monthly payments to creditors.
7. Best of all, you will have peace of mind because you will not owe a large sum of money to anyone.

So what will you use for identification when you have to cash a check? A debit card. A debit card looks much like a credit card, but there are two important differences:

1. When you use a debit card, your checking account treats the purchase like a check because the purchase amount is subtracted from your account. Because you must have money in the bank to use your card, you are prevented from making a lot of charges you cannot afford.

2. If your debit card is lost or stolen, you have greater liability than with a credit card. Before getting a debit card, find out the liability you are assuming.

If you are planning on using credit, do so wisely. Begin by improving your credit rating.

YOUR CREDIT RATING

You have a credit history if you have ever borrowed money for a major purchase or used a major credit card. This information is stored in computers at credit bureaus. Such bureaus sell the information about you to subscribers (businesses or institutions that grant credit) in the form of a credit report. The report will list most but probably not all of the merchants that have offered you credit, and it will show how you repaid them. When you apply for credit, your credit report will identify creditors that you pay on time. If you are past due with any creditor, that will most likely be in your credit report also.

The report will also show whether one or more of your accounts has been referred to a collection agency. Events that are a matter of public record such as bankruptcies, foreclosures, or tax liens are likely to be listed, too.

In addition, your credit report may provide the name of your present employer, former employers, your spouse, and your current and prior addresses. Credit bureaus also maintain a record of all creditors who have requested information about you within the past six months. Prospective employers often check credit records. Life insurance companies usually check credit records, too.

Feel like Big Brother is watching? Well, he is. But don't get paranoid. Turn the tables and take a good look at Big Brother.

Check your credit record. There may be mistakes in your file. When you move to a new location or apply for a major loan, it is a good idea to see your file.

To check your file, get out your telephone directory and look under "credit bureaus." Before a credit bureau will send you a report, however, they will require identification, such as your full name, Social Security number, and your prior address. Ordinarily, a credit bureau will charge you between $5 and $15 for a copy of your report.

If you have applied for credit but have been turned down, federal law allows you to see a copy of your file at no cost within 30 days. The creditor who denied you credit must tell you the name and address of the credit bureau that provided them with a copy of your credit record.

If there is a problem, it is up to you to correct your credit report. Look for the following in your file:

Real life, real answers.

D iane Simpson was hospitalized last year and was unable to work for five months. She quickly exhausted her two weeks of sick pay. Diane fell behind on payments to several creditors. Recently she was denied credit because of negative information in her file. She had the credit bureau insert a statement explaining that because she had been ill she had fallen behind in her payments. Several creditors reevaluated her credit applications and approved them.

☐ Missing information. Chances are information about one or more of your credit accounts is not in your file. The credit bureau will be happy to add that information to your record if you give them the name and address of the lender and information about your accounts.

☐ Incorrect information. Ask the credit bureau to check it out. Wrong information must be removed from your file. If you and a creditor disagree about information in your record, federal law gives you the right to have a hundred-word statement inserted into your record explaining your side of the disagreement.

Because negative information usually remains on your statement for seven years (bankruptcy stays for 10), a statement explaining your side of the story can be helpful.

IMPROVING YOUR CREDIT RATING

You can improve your credit rating. Theoretically, creditors decide if they will grant you credit based on the following:

☐ How you pay your bills.
☐ The amount of your annual income.
☐ The total amount you owe other creditors.
☐ How long you have lived at your present address.
☐ How the creditor could collect from you if you failed to repay.

Although each creditor uses a different system to evaluate

Real life, real answers.

Laura Jensen needed to borrow $5,000 to start her own business. However, because she had no credit history, her bank would not make the loan without collateral. Four years ago, when Laura's dad died, he left her 100 shares of IBM stock. Laura used the stock as collateral and the bank made the loan. Laura understood that when she paid off the loan as agreed, she would get the stock certificates back. If she defaulted on the loan, the bank would sell the stock to pay off the loan. If the proceeds from the sale of the stock were more than the loan balance, Laura would get the difference.

your credit potential, all evaluate your creditworthiness, your capacity to repay, and your character. Given identical information, one creditor may approve your application while a second may turn you down. If you are denied credit, the creditor must tell you exactly why the credit was not granted.

If your credit record is problematic, don't be discouraged. Each creditor evaluates you differently. Some will consider only your most recent credit-paying history.

You can improve your rating by:

1. Becoming current and continuing to pay all creditors on time.

2. Asking someone with a good credit history to cosign your loan. The payment record will become part of your credit history. But if you do not repay the creditor as agreed, the lender can demand immediate payment in full from your cosigner. Be careful.

3. Considering the use of collateral. Collateral is something a lender can use to pay off your loan if you do not repay. Stocks and bonds, or a car you own free and clear, can be used as collateral.

4. Obtaining credit from those who put up the least barriers.

Department stores, for example, may be willing to grant you credit more readily than other sources (and you may even get a gift for applying). Remember, if you are turned down, contact the credit bureau and review a copy of your credit report.

LEARNING TO USE CREDIT

Let's discuss how to use credit effectively. When you apply for a loan, the lender must convert all your costs of borrowing money into one number, the Annual Percentage Rate or APR. This rate includes the cost of your credit report from the credit bureau, the loan application fee, life and disability insurance (which you should probably refuse if you can), and the interest you will pay over the life of the loan.

Federal law requires that the lender tell you what your loan's APR will be before you borrow money. There are two reasons for this: first, so you can easily compare the cost of borrowing money from several lenders by comparing APRs; and second, so you can get a better idea of how expensive borrowing will be.

> **Tip:** When you apply for a loan, a lender cannot discriminate against you on the basis of your sex, race, marital status, religion, national origin, age, or the receipt of public assistance. If you believe you have been discriminated against, contact the office of the Attorney General in your state or the Federal Trade Commission, Consumer Protection Division (6th and Pennsylvania Avenue, N.W., Washington, DC 20580; (202) 326-3238).

If you receive a bill from a creditor that is incorrect, federal law recommends that you respond to the creditor as follows:

☐ Send a letter to the creditor within 60 days of the postmark on the bill. Identify the error and explain why you think the bill is wrong. Pay only the part of the bill that is correct.

☐ While waiting to hear from the creditor, you do not have to pay the disputed amount or any finance charges.

☐ The creditor must acknowledge your letter within 30 days. Either the bill will be corrected or the creditor will send a letter stating the reasons they believe the statement is correct. You will be expected to pay the finance charges that accumulated on the disputed amounts of the bill if you are wrong.

Credit cards (or debit cards) can actually help you manage your money better if you know how to use them. However, if you are an impulsive shopper and rack up hundreds of dollars of bills on your cards each month, these techniques are clearly not for you.

The singular advantages of "plastic" are as follows:

1. Credit or debit cards are useful as identification when you cash a check. Consider, however, using a credit card that does not require an annual fee.

2. When you are away from home, a credit card makes more sense than cash. If a credit card is lost or stolen, your liability is limited to $50 per card (the liability is higher with debit cards). Keep your account numbers and the phone numbers for lost or stolen cards in a safe but accessible place.

3. You may not have to pay for an unsatisfactory purchase made with a credit card if the purchase is $50 or more and is made in your home state. Once you realize the purchase is defective, you should visit the merchant and ask the manager to correct the problem. If the merchant does not, write to the credit card company and ask them to remove the charge from your account. Give the company the following information:

☐ Date of purchase and name and location of merchant.
☐ Amount of the purchase.
☐ Reason that the purchase was not satisfactory.
☐ A description of your visit with the manager who refused to correct the problem.
☐ Copies of sales receipts and warranties (keep the originals).

4. Most credit card companies will not charge you any

interest if you pay off all balances before the next statement date.

The trick to using credit effectively is maintaining control. Don't become a slave to the Credit Monster.

Tip: Carry a single card that is widely accepted. Keeping track of additional cards complicates your bookkeeping and exposes you to greater liability.

CHAPTER VIII

Living debt-free

G etting and staying out of debt is an important objective for the fledgling budgeter. It is a noble goal and will pay you back many times over.

Debts may now demand a large share of the money you earn each month. You may think you don't earn enough to save for future goals, cover your cost of living expenses, and get out of debt. But you do.

A SIX-STEP STRATEGY

To live debt-free will require self-discipline and sacrifice and take time. You can succeed by following this six-step strategy:

1. Admit you have a problem. √
2. Identify the reasons you incur debts. √
3. Stop creating new debts. √
4. Get the whole family involved. √
5. Use a budget. √
6. Work out a plan to eliminate the debt.

You might be tempted to start with Step 6, but you must work through each step consecutively.

Step 1. Admit you have a problem. The hardest part of getting out of debt may be admitting that you have a debt problem. Blaming others for a problem is a sure way to see that the problem is never solved. Only when you can admit to yourself that you alone are responsible for what you owe, will you have the energy, courage, and self-discipline to work your way out of debt.

Step 2. Understand why you are in debt. You will find it much easier to break the debt cycle if you can figure out why you started using credit in the first place. Although there may be many reasons, try to identify the most important ones. First make a list of all your debts.

Lender	Amount Borrowed	Monthly Payment	Interest Rate	Reason for Loan
_____	$ ____	$ _____	____ %	_____
_____	_____	_____	____	_____
_____	_____	_____	____	_____
_____	_____	_____	____	_____
_____	_____	_____	____	_____
_____	_____	_____	____	_____
_____	_____	_____	____	_____
_____	_____	_____	____	_____

Each of the factors listed below identifies a reason that you may have incurred debt. For each loan, insert at least one of the following in the fifth column, Reason for Loan, and place a checkmark on the appropriate line below.

1 ___ Medical bill(s)
2 ___ Home and/or car repairs
3 ___ Clothing
4 ___ Gifts (birthdays, holidays, etc.)
5 ___ Vacations
6 ___ Insurance premiums
7 ___ Taxes

8 ___	Cars
9 ___	Major appliances
10 ___	School tuition
11 ___	Home buying
12 ___	Unemployed
13 ___	Disabled
14 ___	Divorce
15 ___	Other

If you checked 1, your insurance program may need to be evaluated. You may not have been adequately insured. Because insurance premiums vary dramatically, look to improve your coverage without spending much more than you presently do on insurance.

If you checked 1 or 2, you may not be setting aside enough money each month for repairs and medical expenses. Remember to include a repair account in your budget.

There may be several reasons why you checked 3, 4, or 5. More than likely you have not been budgeting effectively and you are easy prey for Madison Avenue tempters. Credit makes it all the more alluring. Your only defense is budgeting. Plan your spending, and then make sure your spending is in line with your planned targets.

If you checked 8 and/or 9, you need to beef up your replacement account.

If you checked 10 and/or 11, you have identified one of the few generally accepted reasons for using credit. When you borrow to get an education, you are investing in yourself or your children; the benefits should remain long after the debt is repaid. If you checked "home buying," you have selected the number one reason why so many families live on a tight budget—buying more house than one can comfortably afford. If your mortgage payment takes more than 28 percent of your take-home pay, you are spending too much on housing.

If you checked 12, 13, or 14, you or your spouse may need

additional education to improve your wage-earning ability. This strategy often requires years to implement. You may want to start by making an appointment with a financial aid officer at a nearby college or university to discuss short-term assistance and long-range strategies.

Step 3. Stop creating debt. To help you keep from creating more debt, you need to take certain steps to make it more difficult for you to borrow. One or more of the following strategies may help.

☑ Cut up all credit cards but one. This hurts. Keep the card with the lowest combination of annual membership fee and annual interest rate. A credit card is usually necessary identification when cashing a check. But try not to use the card unless you cannot pay with cash or a check. Be sure you have enough money in your bank account to cover the charge.

☐ Cancel your overdraft protection. If you have an interest-paying checking account that requires you to keep a minimum balance, you should not need overdraft protection. It is too easy to write checks for more money than you have if you have this false safety net beneath you.

☐ Think long and hard before applying for a home equity loan. If you have one, pay it off. Since the rates are lower than those of credit cards, and the interest is tax deductible, such loans have become extremely popular. A home equity loan makes it too easy to borrow.

☑ Eliminate major impulse purchases by creating and following a budget.

☐ Make a list of all items you and your family want to purchase. Rank the items in order of priority. Next, set up a savings account to purchase the first item on the list. Priorities for items on the list will change. Your family may find it useful to discuss why this happens. As funds are available, purchase the first item on the list.

Step 4. Hold a family council. Explain that the debt problem exists. Ask each member whether he or she is willing to spend the time and energy required to work through a debt elimination program. You need each family member's support to ensure

DEBT-ELIMINATION CALENDAR

Lender: **A** _____ **B** _____ **C** _____ **D** _____ **E** _____

Month

1 _____ _____ _____ _____ _____ _____

2 _____ _____ _____ _____ _____ _____

3 _____ _____ _____ _____ _____ _____

4 _____ _____ _____ _____ _____ _____

5 _____ _____ _____ _____ _____ _____

6 _____ _____ _____ _____ _____ _____

7 _____ _____ _____ _____ _____ _____

8 _____ _____ _____ _____ _____ _____

9 _____ _____ _____ _____ _____ _____

10 _____ _____ _____ _____ _____ _____

11 _____ _____ _____ _____ _____ _____

12 _____ _____ _____ _____ _____ _____

13 _____ _____ _____ _____ _____ _____

14 _____ _____ _____ _____ _____ _____

15 _____ _____ _____ _____ _____ _____

16 _____ _____ _____ _____ _____ _____

17 _____ _____ _____ _____ _____ _____

18 _____ _____ _____ _____ _____ _____

19 _____ _____ _____ _____ _____ _____

20 _____ _____ _____ _____ _____ _____

21 _____ _____ _____ _____ _____ _____

22 _____ _____ _____ _____ _____ _____

23 _____ _____ _____ _____ _____ _____

24 _____ _____ _____ _____ _____ _____

that you will be successful. Everyone must understand the benefits of becoming debt-free and be aware of the challenges ahead. They must also understand that converting to a debt-free lifestyle may be painful initially. Once you stop using credit to prop up your lifestyle, your living standard may decline somewhat for a period of time. But as each creditor is paid off, you will have more cash available for day-to-day expenses.

Step 5. Use a budget. That is what this entire book is about. Do it!

Step 6. Systematically eliminate your consumer debt. Make your own Debt-Elimination Calendar using the form on page 81.

1. On line 1, start with the coming month and continue down the column until you have listed each month twice.

2. On the Lender line, you can put the names of up to five creditors. If you have more than five creditors, add columns as needed. The name you put into slot E should indicate the loan you would like to pay off first (because it has the highest interest rate, is secured, or your reputation is at stake). The lender that goes into slot D represents the loan that you wish to pay off second and so on.

3. Under the lender in slot E, put the regular monthly payment until the loan is paid off. Under the lender in slot D put the regular monthly payment as long as payments are still being made to the lender in slot E. When the first lender in slot E is paid off, add the amount of the payment to lender E to the monthly amount of the payment to lender D (See the *Real life, real answers* story on page 83). This process, known as "folding over," is continued until all loans are paid off. Even though the process will take time, the loans will be paid off eventually, often within two years.

Tip: Some lenders may charge you a penalty if you pay off a loan early. If you have a loan with a prepayment penalty, you have to decide whether paying the penalty is worth getting out of debt as soon as you can. You may

Real life, real answers.

C arl Taylor owed Visa a minimum monthly payment of $50, but felt he could make payments of $110. Sears's payments were $70 a month. He owed his dentist, Dr. Lee, $810, but Dr. Lee was willing to accept payments of $50 a month. Monthly payments on Carl's piano were $75. Monthly car payments were $236. Including his higher payment of $110 to Visa, Carl's total monthly debt repayment amounted to $541. Carl set up the following repayment program to fold over his bills:

		Auto	Piano	Dr. Lee	Sears	Visa	Total
1.	MAY	$236	$75	$50	$70	$110	$541
2.	JUNE	236	75	50	70	110	$541
3.	JULY	236	75	50	70	110	$541
4.	AUG.	236	75	50	70	110	$541
5.	SEPT.	236	75	50	180		$541
6.	OCT.	236	75	50	180		$541
7.	NOV.	236	75	50	180		$541
8.	DEC.	236	75	230			$541
9.	JAN.	236	75	230			$541
10.	FEB.	236	305				$541
11.	MAR.	236	305				$541
12.	APR.	541					$541
13.	MAY	541					$541

decide to pay off the loan with the prepayment penalty last.

The key to Carl Taylor's program is to fold over one loan payment into the next. After the Visa loan is paid off, that monthly payment of $110 is added to the $70 previously paid to Sears. This results in a $180 monthly Sears payment. In less than a year, all loans are paid off except the auto loan. Not all lenders will let you increase the monthly payment, but most will.

Carl's program works well because he had enough income each month to pay each creditor when due. If you do not have the monthly income to pay each creditor his or her full amount

Real life, real answers.

L inda Wallace had a problem but she made sure her two secured creditors were paid on time. She did not have enough income, however, to pay her eight unsecured creditors in full each month. Using the fold-over technique shown in the *Real life, real answers* story on page 83, she worked out a minimum monthly payment she could make to each creditor. Next, Linda called the creditors one by one and explained why she could not pay them the full amount each month. She explained that she had worked out a plan for repaying each of them, and explained the plan in detail. Before calling any creditor she checked and rechecked her budget and her debt repayment program to make sure it would work. She wanted to make sure she could follow the plan exactly before she talked with any creditors. All agreed to her program.

each month, you can use the same format as Carl's with one difference: Reduce the size of some or most of the monthly payments you make to creditors. Some creditors, usually unsecured ones, will let you do this. Secured creditors may not. A secured creditor either has title to the item you are buying or your collateral.

If you get too far behind with any creditor, he or she will either repossess the item sold to you or turn your account over to a collection agency. Most collection agencies pay their collectors on commission. Such an incentive means that the collector who receives your account will do all he or she can to get you to pay. If you find that the collection agency is harassing you, federal law allows you to write the collection agency a letter instructing them never to contact you again. By law, they must abide by your wishes. However, the collection agency may then decide to take you to court. The more money you owe, the more likely your chances that the collection agency will sue you.

CREDIT COUNSELING SERVICES

Maybe you tried to develop a repayment program, but it just didn't work. You may have another alternative. Check with Consumer Credit Counseling Service (CCCS). Their counselors will try to arrange a repayment plan acceptable to you and your creditors. Often that plan includes having the CCCS make the payments to each creditor each month. They also may help you set up a budget.

Check your telephone directory for one of the more than 300 offices of the Consumer Credit Counseling Service. Credit counseling services are offered at little or no cost to you. However, CCCS offices often have a three- to five-week waiting period before they will see you. Also, there are no CCCS offices in small towns.

If you cannot get a satisfactory appointment with a financial counselor at a CCCS beware of other options. Have you ever seen ads for companies that claim they can "erase bad credit" or "remove poor ratings from your credit record"? Such ads are run by credit repair companies. Watch out. These firms will charge you a fee ranging from as little as $25 to amounts exceeding $1,000. They will want you to pay for their services before they do anything. Actually, they cannot do anything for you that you cannot do yourself. They are after the fee. No one can erase negative information from your credit file legally unless the information is incorrect.

If you need help locating an office of the Consumer Credit Counseling Service, contact the National Foundation for Consumer Credit, Inc. (8701 Georgia Avenue, Suite 507, Silver Spring, MD 20910; (301) 589-5600).

BANKRUPTCIES

If you cannot solve your own credit problems and cannot get help from a CCCS, it may be time to visit an attorney who handles bankruptcy. This is an extreme measure and should be used only as a last resort.

You may need to take this drastic action if you are too deeply in debt to meet your daily expenses. Discuss bankruptcy with a lawyer or a legal aid service. There are two types of bankruptcy:

1. Chapter Seven. This is primarily for people with little or no income. You may be forced to sell most of your personal belongings to repay creditors, but you will eventually get your head above the turbulent waters you are in now.

2. Chapter Thirteen. This is available if the amount of your debts is below specified dollar limits and if you have a steady job. Under Chapter Thirteen, a repayment plan is set up so that your creditors are paid directly from your salary.

Once you file for bankruptcy, creditors and collection agencies must leave you alone. Bankruptcy does not relieve you of all financial obligations. You will still be responsible for any debts owed the government as well as alimony and child support.

Another point to consider is that while you are under the control of a bankruptcy court, you must live with the court's budget restraints. If you get a salary increase the trustee might raise the amount you must repay creditors.

For a more thorough discussion of the differences between the two types of bankruptcy, as well as many other aspects of credit, see *How to borrow money and use credit* by Martin Weiss, another book in the *Real life, real answers* series.

You can get out of debt, but first you must get in control of your finances. Effective budgeting is required to gain control. If you truly want to get out of debt, you and your family will need to work through the exercises in this chapter.

Afterword

D eveloping and sticking to a successful spending plan requires commitment, self-discipline, flexibility, time, patience, family involvement, and caution. It should not require complicated recordkeeping, sleepless nights, migraines, family feuds, or heartache.

Going on a budget is like embarking on a fitness program:

☐ Be realistic about what you want to accomplish and what your goals are to be.

☐ Plan your strategy and stick to it.

☐ Be willing to work for your goals.

☐ Be flexible and adjust the program to your needs as they arise.

☐ Understand that life-changing acts require commitment. As you begin to see your goals within reach, acknowledge your success.

Real life, real answers.

The up-to-date library of personal financial information

How to make basic investment decisions
by Neal Ochsner

Planning for a financially secure retirement
by Jim Jenks and Brian Zevnik

How to borrow money and use credit
by Martin Weiss

How to pay for your child's college education
by Chuck Lawliss and Barry McCarty

Your will and estate planning
by Fred Tillman and Susan G. Parker

How to protect your family with insurance
by Virginia Applegarth

The easy family budget
by Jerald W. Mason

How to buy your first home
by Peter Jones

Planning for long-term health care
by Harold Evensky

Financial planning for the two-career family
by Candace E. Trunzo